Purpose of this book

For multiples, family, friends and helping professionals.

To understand the feelings and issues facing people with Multiple Personality Disorder.

To be a vehicle for discussion of these feelings and issues

To help multiples have respect for their diagnosis and treatment needs.

To provide hope that abuse need not overpower the natural drive for healing and wholeness.

About the Author Rachel Downing, MSW, LCSW

I am recovering from Multiple Personality Disorder

I have integrated all personalities and am learning to live my life without MPD.

I was editor of a newsletter for multiples, "Speaking for Our Selves", 1985-1987.

I am a social worker.

I am a mother, a sister and a friend.

Please
Let me
go through
the
door
slowly.
MPD

The beginning
The diagnosis

It can't be true.

I know it is true.

I don't know what is true.

I was not abused.

Maybe I was abused?

At last all these strange thoughts and feelings make sense.

I am scared.

Can I Look Now?

Trusting Myself

Trusting Myselves?

I made it up.
It is not true.
I am bad.

At last someone is
really listening to me.

Who is telling the truth?
who is telling lies?

What is happening to me?

How can I trust myself?

This is a new path.
Therapy
Can I really say anything I want?

Trusting my therapist

Not trusting my therapist.

Stop
confusing me
with your questions.

I AM FINE.

Can you help me?

You can't help me.

Go Away.

Please Listen to me.

My mind is taking care of me.
Always.
Thank you mind
yea mind!

Respect for my mind

I am Learning to respect my mind. It has kept me alive for a long time.

My mind is always working towards healing.

Despite
all the confusion
there is an order
beneath the surface.

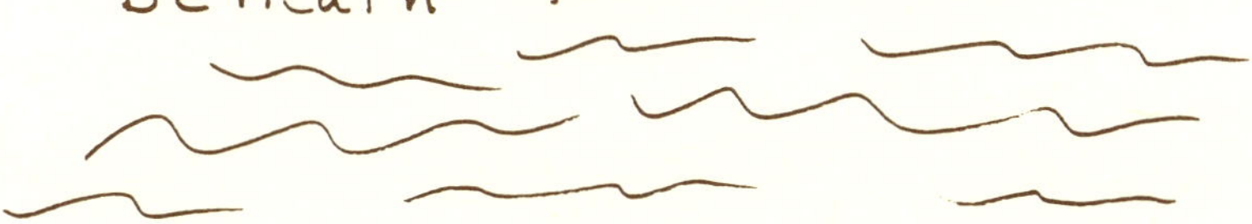

MPD
Spoken
Here
MPD
Welcome
Here
OK
We demand respect and acceptance for Multiple Personality Disorder
MPD
play
room

Acceptance

It is OK to be a person who has Multiple Personality Disorder.

I would have preferred everday Life experiences -- not having this illness.

But I respect my will to Live.
I respect my determined survival in the face of total destruction.

I do not have to Live Like this forever.

Therapy

A Safe Space

Therapy

There are so many
things to Learn.

It is so confusing.
It seems so slow.

Is it really safe to uncover
the secrets hidden from
my self -- my selves?

At Least
a Little safe.

Safe enough. To Begin.

Therapy
hopes
fears
secrets
more
secrets
Secrets
Me
feelings
therapist

Therapy

I am afraid.

I will learn to use the help.

please help me.
don't hurt me.
help, help, help

what helps?

Talking helps.
Sharing helps.

No More Secrets

thoughts
Memories
Me
Personalities
feelings

Getting Comfortable

Learning to tolerate
different, painful,
scary

Memories
thoughts
and
feelings.

Slowly accepting and
making peace with these
hidden parts of
myself.

thoughts and feelings waiting for their turn to come out.
5
4
3
2
1
"Take a number please"
It's my turn

Pacing

I don't have to know
or remember things
until I am ready.

I can
uncover
things
slowly.

Fears
Who will be here next?

Fears

Will someone come out
and just take over?

Will I be gone?
Where will I go?
What will happen to me?

You won't go away.
Everything will be preserved.
With each change you just
get stronger and more whole.

It is all ME!

Understanding

Each personality is here for a reason.

Each has been necessary for my survival.

Each is needed for me to become a whole person.

Are you certain?

Yes

Even scary and mean ones?

Yes

Everyone? YES!

even me?
Not Me!
what about me?
do i count?
I Live in a box
me too?
am I really important?
what about a puppy?

More Acceptance

Notes of welcome and appreciation.

Welcome to ____
Thank you for making yourself known.

Thank You ____________
for helping today by bringing your unique skills and talents to the surface.

"you're welcome"

More Acceptance

So many ways to greet and accept new personalities, parts, ones, etc...

Bulletin Boards

Stuffed Animals

Special Food

Toys

drawing paper and pens

a blanket (very soft)

We All WanT Help
#3

More Therapy

More time.

Weeks, months, years.

More personalities.

How can there possibly be more?

Ones
thoughts
feelings
and
memories.

more and more and more ......

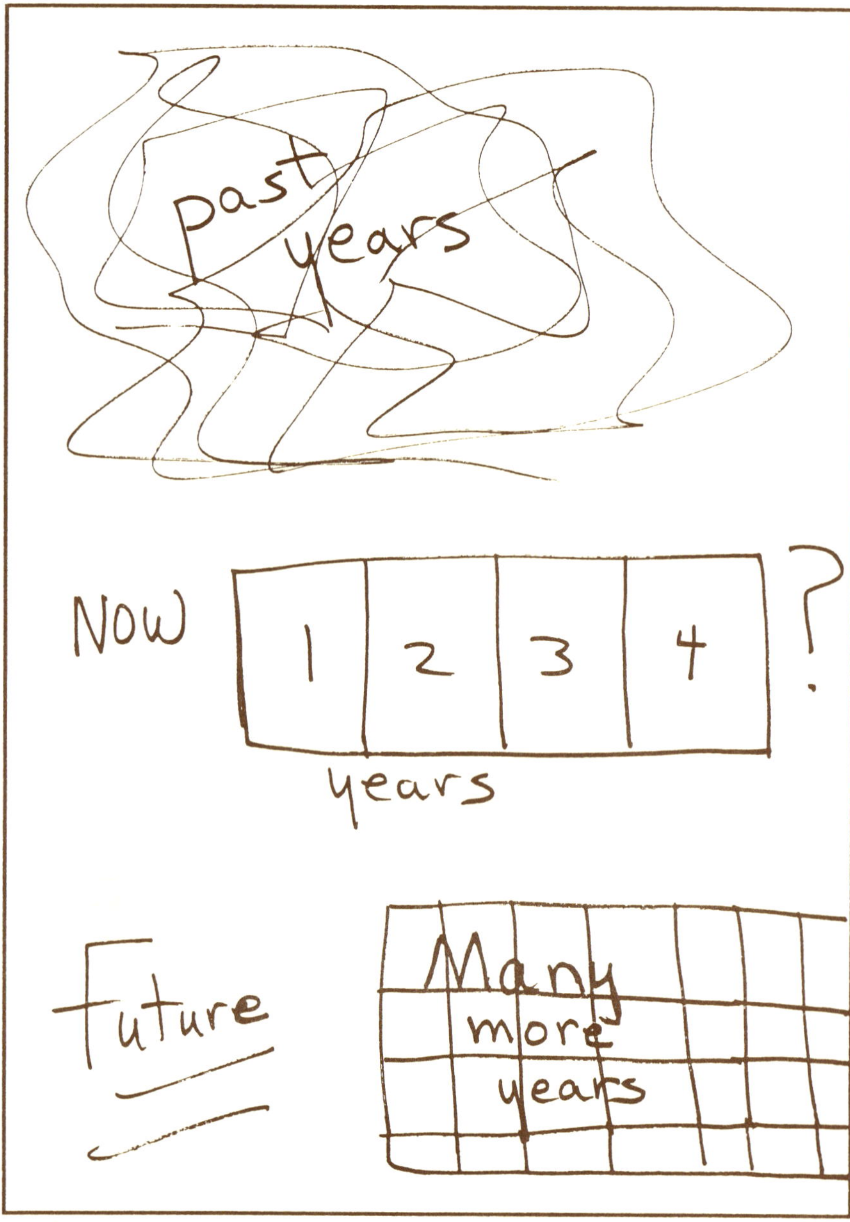
past
years
NOW
1
2
3
4
?
years
Future
Many
more
years

It takes time.

Oh, No!

I have already spent or
Lost too much of my Life.

Will it take years?

yes.

Why?

It took a Long time to
come apart. It will take
time to come together.

OK

I am OK with all thoughts, feelings and memories.

Becoming Whole

It doesn't happen all
at once.

It is a gradual process.

uneven
smooth
rough
pleasant

A natural flow, an internal
process of healing
coming from
communication, trust
understanding and acceptance.

Not rushed or forced.
Natural.

Recovery

No matter where you are on the healing Journey

Beginning

Middle

Ending

Life after MPD

you are OK.

Recovery

The body and the mind
always work towards
healing, health and wholeness.

I believe in me.
I believe in my feelings.
I believe in my mind,

In myself--- myselves.

In the past
In the present
and in the future.

Can I Look Now? Recovery from Multiple Personality Disorder

ORDER FORM

Mail my order to the following:

Name ______________________

____
StreetAddress Apt.#

____
City State ZipCode

____
AreaCode PhoneNumber

For orders outside the United States, please have the money order in American currency.

Make checks payable to: Educational Recovery Communications.

My check or money order for ________ is enclosed.

Expect one to four weeks for delivery.

Number of copies × $5.00 per copy = ____________ Subtotal

Number of copies × $.50 postage and handling per copy = ____________ Subtotal

Maryland residents add 5% sales tax (No. of copies x $.25) = ____________ Subtotal

TOTAL: ____________

Discounts available for orders of 20 or more. Write for information.

Order from:
Educational Recovery Communications
1498M Reisterstown Road, Box 333
Baltimore, MD 21208